AFRICAN WILDLIFE

A photographic safari

SUNBIRD
PUBLISHING

First published 1999

Publisher Dick Wilkins
Editor Sean Fraser
Designer Mandy McKay
Production Manager Andrew de Kock

Reproduction by Unifoto (Pty) Ltd, Cape Town
Printed and bound by Tien Wah Press (Pte) Ltd, Singapore

ISBN 0 62403 788 6

LEFT *A huge haystack-like nest of sociable weavers serves as a safe and comfortable
roosting place for a secretary bird.*
BELOW *The meerkat's tiny body loses heat rapidly during the cold winter nights of
the Kalahari. Meerkats start their day by sunbathing to warm up.*
OPPOSITE *During the dry winter months, waterholes become the centre of activity
for both game and tourists. These Burchell's zebra were part of a continuous
parade of animals visiting this waterhole.*

Introducing African Wildlife

Endowed with a vast landscape of wild open plains, grass-covered savanna, rugged bushveld and arid desert all sweltering under an African sun, the African continent has a diversity of animals spread across a variety of habitats. Once widespread and free ranging, many of the larger mammals are now confined to protected pockets of sanctuary in the national parks and private reserves that serve as custodians of this wildlife heritage. While the Big Five – lion, leopard, rhino, elephant and buffalo – continue to enjoy the most public attention, a broader – and equally spectacular – picture emerges when you consider the others that share the land.

A large herd of elephant (*Loxodonta africana*) crossing the plains is an unforgettable sight. A matriarchal society, the herd consists of a dominant female, her aunts and sisters and offspring. Young bulls leave the herds at puberty to form bachelor groups and return only to mate.

BELOW As mid-morning temperatures soar, an elephant herd hurries to water.

The full-blooded roar of a lion shattering the tranquillity of an African night remains one of the most thrilling bush experiences. Lions (*Panthera leo*) sleep for up to 15 hours a day and, although this behaviour may appear lazy, it is in fact an efficient way of conserving the energy required for hunting. A dominant male controls a huge territory encompassing up to three prides of females and cubs, which, in his absence, are led by a dominant female.

Elusive, mysterious and deadly, the leopard (*Panthera pardus*) is an outstanding hunter and, with a spotted coat that enables it to blend into the dappled shade in and under trees, has an uncanny ability to apparently disappear while in full view. Leopards use trees both as vantage points and resting places and will often drag their prey up into the branches to protect it from scrounging lions or spotted hyaenas.

While it is easy to confuse the white rhino (*Ceratotherium simum*) and black rhino (*Diceros bicornis*), certain physical features and behavioural patterns distinguish the two species. The alternate names provide good clues: square lipped (white) and hook lipped (black). A grazer, the white rhino has a wide, square-shaped muzzle to help it feed on short grasses and low-growing plants, while the black rhino – a browser – has prehensile narrow lips to enable it to strip leaves from branches. Although larger, the white rhino is far more placid and sociable, and is found in groups of up to 10 animals led by a territorial

ABOVE Late evening is the time when large predators, including lion, stir and prepare for the night's hunt.

bull. What the two have in common, however, is their poor eyesight – but finely honed senses of hearing and smell.

The African buffalo (*Syncerus caffer*) – and especially an old, lone bull – is possibly the most unpredictable of Africa's wild creatures, and is often considered the continent's most dangerous. It will charge without provocation, lowering its massive head at the very last minute to toss its hapless victim with a set of impressive horns. Buffalo herds – sometimes numbering hundreds of individuals – are, in contrast, rather placid.

Generally found in and around water, hippos (*Hippopotamus amphibius*) are equally at home on land. On cool days and at night, they come ashore to graze. Despite their rather benign appearance, hippos have massive jaws and fearsome tusk-like teeth that are capable of inflicting terrible injuries – and even death – to both humans and other mammals.

The sleek, elegant cheetah (*Acinonyx jubatus*) is much revered as the fastest land mammal, reaching speeds of over 100 kilometres per hour in a sprint over 400 metres in pursuit of inevitably ill-matched prey. Although in its favour, the cheetah's impressive speed serves as no guarantee, and this naturally timid cat is often deprived of its kill by lion, wild dog and spotted hyaena.

Once deemed mainly scavengers, the spotted hyaena (*Crocuta crocuta*) has proven itself to be an extremely efficient hunter with remarkable stamina and incredibly well-developed senses of smell and hearing. It can smell prey from several kilometres away and easily covers up to 40 kilometres a night, its raucous, manic laughter shattering the still darkness. With massive, powerful jaws and strong forequarters, it is capable of bringing down prey as large as the mighty eland.

BELOW A white rhino calf will accompany its mother for the first two or three years of its life.

Probably the most misunderstood and maligned mammal is the wild dog (*Lycaon pictus*) or, more lyrically, the painted wolf. Persecuted by man and susceptible to domestic canine diseases such as distemper, their numbers have steadily declined and are now found only in protected areas. With strong family bonds, wild dogs – unlike other pack animals – care for the young and infirm of their group. During a hunt, the offspring of the dominant male and female – the only pair in the pack to breed – are left in the care of 'babysitters'. After a successful hunt, the hunters return to the den and regurgitate food for those left behind. Wild dogs have developed a unique hunting system: a few dogs take the lead and, as they tire and drop back, so other dogs move forward to take their places, thus enabling them to outrun their prey.

Predators, however, could not survive without prey. The tallest land mammal, the giraffe (*Giraffa camelopardalis*) has no competition – with the possible exception of elephants – in its search for food. As browsers, they are able to reach the top buds and new growth of trees.

The eland (*Taurotragus oryx*) is the largest of the African antelope, and mature bulls can weigh up to 750 kilograms. Despite its huge size and weight, it is an excellent jumper and may clear a two-metre obstacle with relative ease.

The stately kudu (*Tragelaphus strepsiceros*) is best known for the striking horns of the bull. Used to great effect in their fight over females during the breeding season, they seldom inflict serious injury on each other – although the spirals may become entangled, occasionally resulting in the death of both bulls.

ABOVE The wild dog is one of the most endangered of the predators on the African continent.

While most of the larger mammals occur throughout the continent, some are found almost exclusively in the arid areas and have consequently developed unique adaptations to allow their continued survival in a harsh, inhospitable environment.

With its dramatic colouring, elegant canter and rapier-sharp horns, one such creature is the gemsbok (*Oryx gazella*), or oryx. The gemsbok practises a unique method of thermo-regulation by raising its body temperature to match the ambient temperature. In its nose is a network of small veins through which the warmed blood passes. In this manner, the blood is cooled before it reaches the brain. As with many species found in desert environments, gemsbok are not reliant on surface water and obtain moisture from roots, tubers and, most especially, the *tsamma* melon. Notoriously bad tempered, gemsbok are often seen fighting – sometimes to the death.

ABOVE *The giraffe's 'horns' are in fact bony outgrowths that protrude from the skull.*

Considerably less intimidating is the impala (*Aepyceros melampus*), one of the most common and numerous of Africa's antelopes. Before the start of the breeding season, or rut, year-old males are driven from the herds by territorial rams. These ejected youngsters later join larger bachelor herds. During the rut, the territorial ram will defend his harem, chasing off other males with great speed and loud snorts, and will also engage in horn clashing. These fights sometimes lead to fatal injuries for one of the two males.

But one of the most typical African images is the sight of a herd of up to 1000 springbok (*Antidorcus marsupialis*) crossing the red sands of the Kalahari. Very often, they may be pronking or stotting – leaping into the air, head down, front and back feet almost touching to form an arc, and a crest of white hair raised on the back. This display is often used when fleeing from a cheetah or as a show of fitness when two herds meet up.

The dainty steenbok (*Raphicerus campestris*) also depends on its speed and agility for survival. This timid antelope freezes in the undergrowth when danger threatens and, when noticed, will leap off in small bounds in a zigzag movement.

It is often the smaller creatures that prove to be the highlight of a safari. Arguably the most beautiful of the smaller cats, the caracal (*Felis caracal*), is an elusive, cunning opportunist and a highly efficient hunter. Like the leopard, this tawny cat with black ear tufts is well camouflaged against its surroundings and may also take its prey up into trees.

The distinctive yapping of the black-backed jackal (*Canis mesomelas*) is often an indication of the presence of a leopard – and the possibility of a free meal. The jackals silently follow lion and leopard on the prowl, and wait at a safe distance until the big cats have eaten their fill. Then, in competition with spotted hyaenas and vultures, they fight for the scraps.

Bat-eared foxes (*Otocyon megalotis*), on the other hand, are somewhat more industrious. When foraging, they use their huge ears as radar, listening intently for the sounds of grubs and scorpions, and then dig for their underground prey. Family groups of between four and six live in the burrows that they excavate.

Sharing much the same terrain as burrowing mammals are the reptiles – crocodiles, tortoises, lizards, and snakes. These cold-blooded creatures – usually secretive and shy – have somewhat limited movement but some, like the desert-dwelling snakes and the water monitors that often prefer a wet, marshy environment, skim stealthily across their home terrain.

Of all the creatures on the continent, the snake is undoubtedly the most feared and, for the most part, unjustly so. Many of the regions have only a few venomous reptiles. One of these is the puff adder (*Bitis arietans*) which, although not usually fatal, delivers an extremely painful bite.

Responsible for many human fatalities in rural areas is the Nile crocodile (*Crocodylus niloticus*). Like turtles, the gender of the crocodile embryo is determined exclusively by the temperature of the incubated eggs. High temperatures result in males – whereas the opposite is true of turtles.

The reptilian-looking pangolin (*Manis temmincki*) has its own, unique way to escape danger. When confronted, it curls up into a ball and nothing can penetrate its scale-like plates.

Often ignored on game drives, chacma baboons (*Papio cynocephalus ursinus*) and vervet monkeys (*Cercopithecus aethiops*) can provide endless hours of entertainment for the interested onlooker.

BELOW *This kudu family will need to be especially vigilant as lion frequently hunt at waterholes.*

ABOVE *The chacma baboon is powerfully built, and its most feared natural enemy is the leopard.*

Both species occur in large groups, the baboons led by several dominant males and monkeys by a single dominant male. Adult males take on sentry duty and, in the case of baboons, will even chase off a leopard, their most feared enemy. Both species eat roots, fruit, shoots, locusts and eggs, and baboons are also known to take hares and even small antelope. Mutual grooming is an important daily ritual and serves to strengthen bonds within the troop.

With such a wide range of microclimates and habitats spread across the continent, Africa is home to an enormous diversity of birdlife. Across the savanna soar eagles and other raptors while, from the treetops watch wide-eyed owls, and along its water courses stroll waterbirds, feeding from the marshy banks on which they nest.

One of the sounds most commonly associated with the great continent is the distinctive call of the African fish eagle (*Haliaeetus vocifer*), as it swoops down from its perch to snatch a fish from the water below.

Also often found around water courses, but just as at home in thornveld, open woodland and coastal forest, are the kingfishers. Just as colourful are the rollers, bee-eaters and sunbirds, all of which boast equally brilliant plumage. These birds all have their own, particular call, but few are as distinctive as the hoot of the owl. Owls, from the giant eagle owl (*Bubo lacteus*) to the small pearlspotted owl (*Glaucidium capense*), hunt by night.

As darkness falls, entirely different mammals emerge from underground shelters and tree hollows to begin their nightly quest for survival.

Despite poor eyesight, the solitary, secretive aardvark (*Orycteropus afer*) has excellent senses of hearing and smell to detect its prey. It uses its extremely strong nails to dig into the hardest of grounds, and its long, sticky tongue of about 20 centimetres extends to twice that length to scoop up the ants and termites that constitute its diet.

Meerkats (*Suricata suricatta*), or suricates, are enchanting creatures: curious, intelligent, and sociable. As their tiny frames lose body heat rapidly, they sunbathe at the entrance to their burrow on a chilly morning, grooming, cuddling and playing before setting off to forage. Adults stand sentry duty on termite mounds, bushes and branches, constantly alert to the approach of predators. Meerkats themselves feed on geckos, lizards, spiders and the like, and have a unique tolerance for snake and scorpion venom.

Dwarf mongooses (*Helogale parvula*) – playful, inquisitive and sociable – are a delight to observe. Like the larger banded mongoose (*Mungos mungo*), they have a unique way of eating eggs. An egg is held in the front paws and tossed backwards through the hind legs at a stone until it breaks.

The ground squirrel (*Xerus inauris*) is another survivor of the arid parts, and uses its huge bushy tail to shade itself from the fierce summer sun. Although its main foods are roots, seeds and bulbs, the ground squirrel may – considering its living conditions – also take its water requirements from the wild cucumber.

Privileged as we are to have such a huge diversity of natural life, it is the duty and obligation of every individual to protect and conserve this heritage for future generations. This can be done by supporting the conservation bodies that do so much to safeguard the continued existence of our unique wildlife and wilderness areas.

BELOW *Resembling a remnant from the dinosaur age, the Nile crocodile has changed little in the last 65 million years.*

LEFT Elephants (*Loxodonta africana*) are extremely protective of their young and females will not hesitate to chase away any intruder they perceive as a threat.

ABOVE Among the most intelligent of Africa's game, elephants derive great pleasure from play activity in and around waterholes.

OPPOSITE Elephants form a matriarchal society comprising female relatives of the matriarch. Young males, upon reaching puberty, are expelled from the herd and will only briefly rejoin the females for breeding purposes.

OVERLEAF LEFT Adult elephants frequently show affection to other members of the herd by using their trunks in tactile expression.

OVERLEAF RIGHT Large bulls may reach a height of four metres and weigh up to 6500 kilograms. Although they normally move at a leisurely stroll, elephants can, when threatened, achieve speeds in excess of 35 kilometres per hour.

ABOVE At times, the youngsters becomes overly exuberant – to the irritation of the more dignified adults who will not hesitate to reprimand them.

OPPOSITE TOP LEFT The calves' playful gambolling is often accompanied by shrill shrieks of pleasure or anger as one gets the upper hand.

OPPOSITE BOTTOM LEFT Calves are born after a 22-month gestation and weigh about 120 kilograms at birth. Should the mother die, the calf may be nursed by another mother in the herd.

OPPOSITE RIGHT Young elephants are vulnerable to predation by lions and remain close to their mothers at all times.

ABOVE AND RIGHT Almost dwarfed by the huge Ana trees in Kaokoland, the desert-dwelling elephants of the region have adapted to feed without destroying their food supplies. Only a few branches are broken off and these are consumed before the elephants move on.
OPPOSITE Water is extremely scarce in this harsh, arid environment. The elephant herds of Kaokoland may travel great distances across the moon-like landscape to reach water. While in most areas elephants drink up to 160 litres a day, these will only drink every two to three days.

TOP LEFT Lion (*Panthera leo*) have no breeding season. Courtship is instigated by either the male or the female and, during this period, the male stays close to the lioness at all times, mating every fifteen minutes over several days.

LEFT A lioness usually has her first litter at about three-and-a-half years of age. She leaves the pride to give birth and only returns when her cubs are about six weeks old. Litters average two to four cubs, although exceptions of up to six have been recorded.

ABOVE Like a domestic cat, lions lap at the water and, as a result, spend a long time drinking their fill.

OPPOSITE The long mane of the adult male may vary from a pale tawny colour to black, and the hair can reach a length of about sixteen centimetres.

PREVIOUS PAGE LEFT At dusk, a large male roars to proclaim his territory, warning intruders to keep their distance.

PREVIOUS PAGE RIGHT During the hot summer months, lion are active mostly at night. With the approach of dawn, these lionesses will seek a shady spot to rest up so that they may conserve energy for the hunt.

LEFT, BELOW LEFT AND BELOW Lion cubs are vulnerable to predation by spotted hyaena, leopard and lion from other prides. For protection, they remain close to the adults in the pride.

OPPOSITE A fallen tree makes an ideal vantage point for lion cubs to enjoy a game of rough-and-tumble. Cubs will be dependent on their mother for the first two years or so, and need to be almost fully grown before they have sufficient strength and skill to participate in a hunt.

LEFT An exceptionally skilled and intelligent hunter, the prey of the leopard (*Panthera pardus*) ranges from antelope – often twice its size – to hares, mice and even insects.
ABOVE Leopards hunt with great stealth and skill.
OPPOSITE Leopards are expert climbers and may even hide in a tree from which it will then ambush its prey.

PREVIOUS PAGES The leopard's coat provides good camouflage, and the predator is almost invisible in dappled light.

LEFT A mature male can weigh as much as 80 kilograms and has a massive head with powerful jaws. Leading a solitary existence, males join the females solely for courtship.

BELOW Leopards are able to hunt with stealth on rocky and often inhospitable terrain. Where not persecuted, leopards are often active during cool, overcast days. Outside of conservation areas – where they may encounter persecution by humans – they are shy and strictly nocturnal.

OPPOSITE The spot pattern above the leopard's whiskers is unique to each individual, very much like the fingerprints of humans. These patterns are often used by researchers for identification of individual animals.

ABOVE White rhinos (*Ceratotherium simum*) often wallow in muddy pools in the hot summer months. As well as cooling them, the mud provides a protective layer against skin parasites. It is not unusual to see terrapins picking ticks and other parasites off the rhino's hide as it wallows in the water.

TOP RIGHT AND RIGHT The white rhino has a poorly developed sense of sight but excellent hearing capabilities. Oxpeckers often accompany rhino and, apart from helping to rid them of skin parasites, these birds also act as an early warning system, compensating for the rhino's poor eyesight.

OPPOSITE LEFT AND RIGHT The two rhino species may be easily distinguished by identifying physical features. The black rhino (*Diceros bicornis*, right) has a narrow muzzle with a prehensile lip that enables it to browse on thorny acacia trees, while the white rhino (left) has a square muzzle ideally suited for grazing. The white rhino is a sociable, placid animal often found in large groups while, in contrast, the solitary black rhino – which does not have a fixed territory – has a rather volatile temperament and is prone to charge at the slightest provocation.

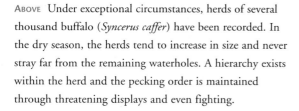

ABOVE Under exceptional circumstances, herds of several thousand buffalo (*Syncerus caffer*) have been recorded. In the dry season, the herds tend to increase in size and never stray far from the remaining waterholes. A hierarchy exists within the herd and the pecking order is maintained through threatening displays and even fighting.

ABOVE Buffalo usually congregate at waterholes in the early morning and late afternoon, and graze on thick clumps of grass. They have an efficient digestive system that can cope with tall, coarse grass unpalatable to most other animals. The presence of buffalo is important to other grazers as the herds trample old stands of grass, thereby encouraging fresh growth.

OPPOSITE The cow-like appearance of the buffalo is deceptive. Lone bulls, in particular, are cunning and aggressive and much feared in the old days of African hunting safaris. The heavy boss (a hard, cap-like structure at the base of the horns) may deflect or even stop a rifle bullet, making a charging buffalo a formidable opponent.

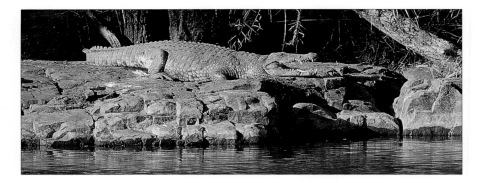

LEFT The Nile crocodile (*Crocodylus niloticus*) is Africa's largest reptile. Gaping – its wide snout open – allows the crocodile to control its temperature. By doing so, the body is cooled by evaporation of moisture through the mouth.

LEFT CENTRE Although sometimes found on land, the crocodile is more at home in an aquatic habitat where a gentle ripple on the water's surface is usually the only indication of its presence.

BOTTOM LEFT The eyes are covered by a protective, transparent membrane allowing the crocodile to follow its prey underwater. Situated just behind the eye is the external ear covered by a flap of skin that prevents intake of water when the crocodile dives.

BELOW After an incubation period of nearly three months, the female carefully scratches the sand off the eggs at the nest. With great care, she gently scoops the hatchlings into her mouth and transports them to a quiet pool.

OPPOSITE Under exceptional circumstances, Nile crocodiles may reach 1000 kilograms. Favouring large rivers, lakes and swamps, they may also be found in river mouths and estuaries. Subject to heavy hunting pressure in the past, viable populations are now mainly restricted to game reserves and other protected areas.

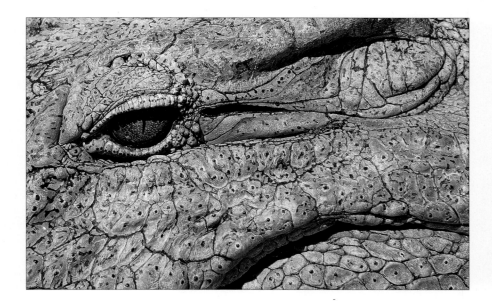

ABOVE LEFT Although hippos (*Hippopotamus amphibius*) come ashore at night to graze, most of the day is spent partially submerged in pools or rivers as their hairless skin is susceptible to sunburn. Adult hippos may walk on the bottom in deep water and can remain underwater for up to six minutes a a time.

LEFT AND ABOVE When confronted or threatened, a hippo will charge through the water in an attempt to chase off the intruder. Females with young are often particularly aggressive and are capable of overturning a small boat. Displays of aggression take the form of vigorous head shaking with the mouth wide open showing impressive canines.

OPPOSITE Although a matriarchal society, the bull leads the herd on foraging expeditions. Young bulls, on reaching maturity, are forced from the herd by violent means. During the mating season, fighting may reach intense proportions as the bull drives off intruders. Most encounters are, however, ritualized displays where little if any serious damage is inflicted.

ABOVE The cheetah (*Acinonyx jubatus*) gives birth to up to five cubs in a well-secluded spot, usually in tall grass. Vulnerable to predation by lion, spotted hyaena, leopard and even large raptors, the mother regularly moves the cubs to a new location to avoid detection. The cubs walk at the age of three weeks and, after six weeks, are strong enough to follow their mother.

OPPOSITE The threat display shown here is purely bluster as cheetah are, by nature, timid and non-aggressive animals that will avoid confrontation rather than instigate it. They are often chased off their kills by other predators and even a band of black-backed jackals has been known to force a cheetah to abandon its meal.

LEFT AND BOTTOM LEFT The hyaena family is represented by only three species in Africa. The spotted hyaena (*Crocuta crocuta*, left), with a wide distribution in sub Saharan Africa, the brown hyaena (*Hyaena brunnea*, bottom left), which is endemic to the dry western area of southern Africa, and the striped hyaena (*H. hyaena*) that occurs from central Tanzania northwards.

BELOW Although spotted hyaena cubs are well developed at birth, their appearance is quite different to the adults as their fur is dark brown to black. It is only after four months that the characteristic spots start to appear.

OPPOSITE As well as preying on larger herbivores and scavenging lion kills, spotted hyaena may also eat smaller prey such as birds and small mammals.

OPPOSITE One of Africa's most endangered species, the African wild dog (*Lycaon pictus*) is now restricted to protected areas. Wild dog packs do not defend territories but have huge home ranges exceeding several thousand square kilometres with the result that few game reserves are large enough to afford them protection.

TOP, ABOVE AND RIGHT In a highly complex social structure, only the alpha male and female breed. Disused antbear holes are most often used as breeding dens where all members of the pack take turns in guarding the pups. After a successful hunt, adult wild dogs regurgitate food that is then fed to the pups and 'babysitters'.

LEFT The placid and gentle giraffe (*Giraffa camelopardalis giraffa*) has very good eye-sight, keen hearing and a good sense of smell. Averaging five metres in height, adult males are mainly solitary but may wander from one herd to the next. Although the giraffe generally benefits from the cleansing of skin parasites by oxpeckers, the birds may irritate a cut or graze thus preventing the wound from healing completely.

ABOVE When drinking, a series of special valves in the jugular vein prevent blood from rushing too quickly to the giraffe's head. Surprisingly, the giraffe has only seven neck vertebrae – the same number as most other mammals – and the exceptionally long neck is simply because each bone is elongated.

OPPOSITE After a gestation period of 15 months, the female gives birth standing up. When the calf drops to the ground, the umbilical cord is broken. Within an hour, the calf is able to stand and begin suckling. It is weaned after seven months and will leave its mother after 14 months.

LEFT The Cape mountain zebra (*Equus zebra zebra*, left) is confined to the mountains of the southern Cape. This rare and endangered animal is smaller than the Burchell's, or plains zebra (*E. burchelli*, below); it has no shadow stripes on its hindquarters and the black bands do not encircle its belly.

BELOW AND OPPOSITE The Burchell's zebra is more likely to associate with other animals, in particular the blue wildebeest (*Connochaetes taurinus*). Extremely vocal – especially at waterholes – squabbling often breaks out among individuals in the herd. They enjoy frequent dust baths, which may result in their white stripes becoming discoloured.

ABOVE Found primarily in savanna woodland, blue wildebeest can, however, tolerate much drier conditions than Burchell's zebra. The rut takes place during April and the young brown-coloured calves are born in summer. Herds, often seen with springbok and Burchell's zebra, may number more than a thousand and, in the Serengeti, more than a million individuals migrate between seasonal feeding and watering grounds.

OPPOSITE LEFT Where water is abundantly available, blue wildebeest tend to drink about twice a day, but in the very dry areas – such as the Kalahari – they are able to survive without water for considerably longer periods.

OPPOSITE RIGHT Blue wildebeest flourish in conditions where short, nutritious grass is abundant. When only very long grass is available – such as during wet cycles – their numbers decline.

LEFT, ABOVE AND OPPOSITE Africa's most impressive antelope, the eland (*Taurotragus oryx*) prefers dry conditions and avoids forests. Largely nomadic, eland often migrate in search of food. Although they will drink if water is available, they take all the moisture they need from roots, tubers and melons. Mainly browsers, they will feed on the fresh, tender, grass shoots that emerge after rain. Naturally shy, eland tend to run away – thus avoiding confrontation with intruders.

OPPOSITE, BELOW AND RIGHT Stately and graceful, the greater kudu (*Tragelaphus strepsiceros*) are predominantly savanna woodland animals. Almost exclusively browsers, they are able to feed on most plant species – even those that may be poisonous to other browsers. To avoid a build-up of toxins, they feed briefly on each plant before moving on to the next one. Kudu are found in small groups of up to 10 animals and, during the rut, intense fighting often erupts between competing bulls, all of which sport the distinctive spiralled horns. A young bull (opposite) spends several years as a bachelor before it is strong enough to challenge a dominant male for access to a breeding herd. The sexes differ in appearance. The mane of the cow (right) reaches only as far as the shoulder, while the bull's extends further down his back and he boasts a long fringe on the throat and neck. The kudu's stripes and facial markings are unique to the individual and are thus often used by reseachers for identification purposes.

LEFT AND ABOVE A striking characteristic of the waterbuck (*Kobus ellipsiprymus*) is the white ring on the rump. This feature is present in both sexes, but only the male carries the forward-swept horns that are used effectively in defence as well as fighting.

OPPOSITE A gregarious species, waterbuck usually occur in small groups of between six and 12 animals. They need to drink daily and are always found close to water. When pursued, waterbuck may seek the safety of deep water and submerge themselves until only their nostrils are visible above the surface. Unlike most other antelope species, they appear to show little fear of crocodiles.

OPPOSITE Sable (*Hippotragus niger*) are an elegant and aloof species, reluctant to share the company of other antelope species. They prefer open savanna woodlands with stands of medium to tall grass, with a constant supply of water nearby. In common with many antelope, a female sable will leave the herd shortly before giving birth and conceal her calf for the first few days until it is strong enough to follow the herd.

BELOW AND RIGHT Nyala (*Tragelaphus angansi*) show striking differences between the sexes. The male has a long, shaggy, dark coat, while the females are without horns and have a rich, tawny coat with distinctive white stripes. Mainly browsers, nyala may also eat fruit and seed pods. In game reserves, they generally become habituated to the presence of vehicles, providing ideal game-viewing opportunities. In hunting areas, they are exceedingly shy – to the extent that they were once considered strictly nocturnal. Ewes and calves are often found in the company of impala, while older males are either solitary or travel in pairs.

ABOVE A specialised antelope of the hot, dry regions, the gemsbok (*Oryx gazella*), or oryx, has a special adaptation to cope with such harsh conditions. It allows its body temperature to rise but cools the blood flowing to the brain by first passing it through a fine network of veins located around the nose. Although hunted by lions, the gemsbok, with its thick neck, sturdy build and rapier horns (common to both sexes), is a formidable opponent and will bravely fight off attack by predators.

ABOVE AND RIGHT Gemsbok are able to take all their moisture requirements from *tsamma* melons and roots and tubers that they dig up. They will, however, utilise drinking sources where available. A strict hierarchy exists within the herd and gemsbok are probably seen fighting more frequently than any other antelope species.

LEFT Wide ranging over eastern and southern Africa, impala (*Aepyceros melampus*) are an adaptable species. They are considered mixed feeders as they browse and graze, allowing them to prosper in areas that have been heavily utilised by other species. This young ram will be driven from the herd at the start of the next rut. The rut occurs during autumn when the dominant males establish territories, while the other males live apart in bachelor herds.

BOTTOM LEFT During the rut, fighting is common between competing males.

BELOW Impala are the principal prey species of leopard, cheetah and wild dog and are also often taken by lion. Drinking time at the waterhole leaves them particularly vulnerable to predation.

OPPOSITE Mutual grooming, or allogrooming, enables individuals to be groomed in difficult-to-reach places.

LEFT Red hartebeest (*Alcelaphus buselaphus caama*) are among the most difficult antelope species for predators to catch. As well as being alert and wary, they are swift runners with plenty of stamina, and are able to maintain speeds of up to 65 kilometres per hour. The red-brown coat has a glossy sheen, appearing almost iridescent in bright sunlight.

ABOVE Found only in the *fynbos* habitat of the southwestern Cape, the bontebok (*Damaliscus dorcas dorcas*) was hunted almost to extinction by the 1830s. Thanks to the efforts of a few conservation-minded farmers and the then National Parks Board, numbers have grown considerably from the tiny remnant population, and bontebok have been success-fully reintroduced to many reserves and farms.

OPPOSITE The bontebok and blesbok (*Damaliscus dorcas phillipsi*, opposite) are, in fact, subspecies of the same animal. Blesbok have a rather wider distribution, occurring widely in the highlying regions of South Africa.

OPPOSITE In the late 1800s, congregations of springbok (*Antidorcas marsupialis*) – numbering hundreds of thousands – migrated from the Kalahari to the Cape in search of food. Huge 'treks' are now a thing of the past as fences block the traditional routes, but herds of several hundred are still seen.

BELOW Springbok both graze and browse and can satisfy all their moisture requirements from their food, but when water is available they will make good use of it.

RIGHT AND BOTTOM RIGHT Males are territorial, but generally only defend territories during the breeding season. Their grunting bellow during the rut is a familiar sound after the season's first rains. Fighting can break out between breeding males. Among bachelor herds, sparring is more playful.

LEFT The agile grey rhebok (*Pelea capreolus*) favour rocky mountain terrain with good grass cover. When fleeing, they – like the reedbuck – use the characteristic rocking-horse movement and display the white underside of the tail as a flag to the rest of the herd.

BOTTOM LEFT AND BELOW Bushbuck (*Tragelaphus scriptus*) are widely distributed in suitable riverine or other densely covered habitats in the sub-Saharan region. They tend to lie up in thick cover during the day and are active only in early morning and late afternoon. Bushbuck browse mainly during the night and feed on a variety of shoots, seed pods and leaves, as well as fresh new grass. As their preferred habitat is often shared with the leopard, they regularly fall prey to this carnivore. The female (bottom left) is pale and small, and the male (below) has a dark coat and a set of horns.

OPPOSITE The reedbuck (*Redunca arundinum*) is found in stands of reeds and tall grass near water. Pairs occupying territories communicate through signals including various whistling calls.

ABOVE AND OPPOSITE The pattern and colour of the coat of the sleek and elegant serval (*Leptailurus serval*) resembles, to a certain degree, that of the cheetah. As it is usually found in the dense growth of grass and reeds near water or on the forest edges, the serval is relatively widely distributed across the continent. Mainly nocturnal and solitary, males and females only join up to mate during the breeding season. After a gestation period of between 70 and 80 days, the female serval gives birth to between one and three kittens during the summer months, and they will remain with her until they reach maturity. Guinea fowl, hares and cane rats are the prey most commonly taken by the serval.

LEFT Similar to the domestic cat, the African wild cat (*Felis silvestri*) can be identified by the rufous colour of the backs of their ears, striped legs and short double-banded tail. While absent from true desert areas, the overall colour of the coat varies from light, sandy grey in dry areas to dark grey in the wetter regions. Largely nocturnal and naturally shy, the African wild cat can be spotted in the early mornings or late afternoons in overcast weather conditions.

ABOVE AND OPPOSITE In common with the smaller cat species, the caracal (*Caracal caracal*) is largely nocturnal and solitary. In protected areas, it sometimes hunts during the day but is seldom seen due to its secretive nature and its colouring that enables it to blend into its surroundings. A remarkably beautiful cat with characteristic black ear tufts, the caracal is a superb and savage hunter. Like the leopard, it may drag its prey into a tree to keep it away from other predators. Its preferred prey species are smaller antelope – such as steenbok – dassies, hares, birds and the young of larger antelope.

OPPOSITE AND RIGHT A true fox, the Cape fox (*Vulpes chama*) is only found in open grassland or semi-desert scrub near rocky outcrops in southern Africa. Mainly nocturnal and solitary, they lie up in thickets or holes, emerging at sunset to forage.

ABOVE The cheeky and cunning black-backed jackal (*Canis mesomelas*) regularly mobs its main enemy, the leopard, and will scavenge food from lion, hyaena and cheetah kills. They are also great opportunists and skilful hunters of smaller prey.

TOP LEFT AND LEFT Slightly larger than a jackal and similar in appearance to the hyaena, the aardwolf (*Proteles cristatus*) consequently met with widespread persecution in the past. They are, however, shy, harmless insectivores that feed mainly on harvester termites, from which they usually obtain all their moisture requirements. The only times they have been observed drinking has been during long, cold spells when there has been no termite activity. Up to three cubs are born in summer and are tended by the female while still in the burrow. The male will only join them once they are active outside the den.

ABOVE Seasonal breeders, the pups of the bat-eared fox (*Otocyon megalotis*) are born in summer when, after good rains, there is an abundance of food for the parents. The tiny pups are very vulnerable and often become an easy meal for an eagle or jackal. Should she detect danger, the mother will try to move the pups to another, safer burrow system.

OPPOSITE Bat-eared fox occur mainly in hot, dry areas where, during the summer months, searing temperatures force them to become nocturnal. In the cool of winter, they are active by day. As indicated by their huge ears, they have a remarkable sense of hearing, and are capable of detecting the slightest movements of their underground prey of grubs, geckos and bugs.

TOP LEFT AND LEFT The more brightly coloured water monitor (*Varanus niloticus*) is Africa's largest lizard, reaching a maximum length of two metres. Common in major river systems, it is a strong swimmer using its long tapering tail for propulsion.

ABOVE Smaller than the water monitor, the rock monitor (*V. albigularis*) generally lives in a tunnel dug under rock overhangs, a rock crack, abandoned burrow or, as shown here, a hole in a tree, where they hibernate in winter.

OPPOSITE The water monitor's main diet consists of crabs and mussels but they also forage for fish and frogs in freshwater pools. The specimen shown here has scavenged a large catfish that it dragged ashore before starting to feed. They also raid birds' nests and even unattended crocodile nests for eggs – even though the crocodile is also one of the main predators of the water monitor.

LEFT The back of the head of the common night adder (*Causus rhombeatus*) displays the characteristic dark 'V' shape. Active only under cover of darkness. it is aggressive and quick to bite.

ABOVE The fairly common yellow Cape cobra (*Naja nivea*) is equally aggressive, and is responsible for a large number of snakebite fatalities.

OPPOSITE Active as darkness falls, the sluggish puff adder (*Bitis arietans*) ambushes rodents and small birds. The bite is not usually fatal to humans but is nevertheless painful.

OVERLEAF LEFT The small Péringuey's or side-winding adder (*B. péringueyi*), found in the Namib dunes, ambushes prey by burrowing into the sand, leaving only its eyes exposed.

OVERLEAF RIGHT Also a creature of the desert region, the Namaqua chameleon (*Chamaeleo namaquensis*) is terrestrial, feeding on insects, lizards and even small snakes.

ABOVE Although widespread, Temminck's pangolin (*Manis temmincki*) is shy, solitary and nocturnal and seldom seen. Covered in horny plates, it rolls up into a tight ball when disturbed. The scales or plates are sharp and serrated and can seriously injure would-be attackers. Feeding on ants and termites, this curious creature moves by shuffling along on its hind limbs.

OPPOSITE When threatened, the porcupine (*Hystrix africaeaustralis*) raises its quills and rattles them to frighten off the assault. As a last resort, it will back into its attacker and the loose quills often become embedded in the throat or lower face of the assailant causing festering wounds that can lead to starvation and death of the attacking lion or leopard.

LEFT, BELOW AND BOTTOM Troops of chacma baboon (*Papio cynocephalus ursinus*) can consist of up to 100 animals. Several dominant males lead the troop and initiate mutual grooming (bottom), while young baboons (left), although lovingly treated by the group, are strictly disciplined. There is lots of squabbling among younger males, but these arguments are not serious and are halted by older males. Vicious fighting between competing males may, however, end in death. Baboons sometimes travel great distances to forage and will even cross rivers (below) to feed.

OPPOSITE Roots, tubers, wild fruit, insects and scorpions form part of the chacma baboon's diet. These intelligent creatures are quick to exploit available food sources and this individual has learnt to uproot water lilies growing on the edge of a pan to reach the succulent tubers.

ABOVE Vervet monkeys (*Cercopithecus aethiops*) are highly strung, nervous and very excitable. Their largely vegetarian diet consists of leaves, wild fruit, flowers, seeds and, as shown in the above photograph, tubers. They will not, however, pass up a chance for a meatier snack and will also eat spiders, locusts and eggs.

OPPOSITE Juvenile vervet monkeys tend to associate with others of the same age, and their noisy and energetic play is part of the learning process. Grooming (bottom left) serves to strengthen bonds between females and young. Senior members sleep in a group in rocky areas or in the branches of trees, while individuals with a lower status form a separate group.

LEFT, TOP AND ABOVE The upper tusks of the warthog (*Phacochoerus africanus*) are used for digging and the lower ones for defence and fighting. When feeding, they kneel on their forelegs to reach succulent grass shoots, roots, tubers and wild fruit. Warthogs wallow in mud as this helps to keep them cool and rids the skin of parasites.

OPPOSITE The nocturnal bushpig (*Potamochoerus larvatus*) lives in dense cover near water, emerging at night to forage. Apart from providing milk for her three to four piglets, the sow leaves the responsibility of raising them to the dominant boar.

TOP LEFT The tiny Damara dik dik (*Madoqua kirki*) is shy and elusive and, unlike other small antelope, does not have scent glands between its hooves. To mark territory, they dig in their latrines before walking around their borders.

LEFT The steenbok (*Raphicerus campestris*) feeds mainly in the cool morning and afternoon, resting during the heat of the day. When fleeing, it uses slight zigzag movements, giving short leaps to clear ground quicker. It stops to look back regularly – an action that may prove fatal.

ABOVE Found in hilly areas, the klipspringer (*Oreotragus oreotragus*) may often be seen poised on a rock. A unique feature is that the hairs of its coat are hollow, giving the animal better insulation to both hot and cold conditions.

OPPOSITE Klipspringers are found in small family groups or in pairs, although they are sometimes solitary. Independent of water, they sometimes browse in the surrounding flatter areas and, when disturbed, speedily return to their rocky terrain. Klipspringer mark territories by rubbing the pre-orbital gland situated just in front of the eye on twigs or shrubs.

OPPOSITE The common duiker (*Sylvicapra grimmia*) thrives in most areas, as long as there is some bush to provide shelter and food.

BELOW Sharpe's grysbok (*Raphicerus sharpei*) favours low-growing shrub in the eastern region.

BOTTOM Red duiker (*Cephalophus natalensis*) are found in dense thickets of the eastern regions.

RIGHT The Cape grysbok (*Raphicerus melanotis*) is a specialist of the scrub bush of the southern and southwestern tip of the continent.

TOP LEFT A widespread and common bird of prey, the tawny eagle (*Aquila rapex*) may scavenge carrion as well as hunt for live prey. Often seen perched high in a tree, the tawny eagle can at times be difficult to identify as individuals may vary in colour from pale cream to dark brown.

LEFT The martial eagle (*Polemaetus bellicosus*) is among the most impressive of Africa's raptors. This huge bird is quite capable of catching mammals up to the size of a common duiker.

ABOVE Now confined mainly to southern Africa's larger game reserves, the bateleur (*Terathopius ecaudatus*) has a characteristic delta wing profile and appears almost tailless in flight.

OPPOSITE At times, hundreds of whitebacked vultures (*Trigonoceps occipitalis*) may gather at a carcass. Although the bare neck might appear ugly to the human eye, it prevents plumage from becoming soiled with blood as the vulture feeds.

LEFT The African fish eagle (*Haliaeetus vocifer*) mainly hunts by swooping down to take live fish from the water, but will also take carrion – such as this large catfish – if the opportunity arises.

BELOW Preening is important for the maintenance of feathers, and this little egret (*Egretta garzetta*) may be seeking to relieve irritation from a feather mite.

OPPOSITE At the end of the dry season, huge flocks of white pelicans (*Pelecanus onocrotalus*) gather when fish stocks are concentrated in the few remaining pans. The appetite of these voracious birds is such that they rapidly fish out smaller pans requiring them to move on after a few days.

LEFT A member of the widow family, the red bishop (*Euplectes orix*) adds a splash of colour to the reeds or tall grass in which it breeds. A gregarious species, the males lose their bright plumage in winter and closely resemble the rather drab females.

ABOVE In common with many of Africa's kingfishers, the brownhooded kingfisher (*Halcyon albiventris*) is not dependent on water and may often be spotted hunting insects from a perch in the bushveld.

OPPOSITE LEFT The longclaw family is mainly associated with grassland and wetlands, but the yellow-throated longclaw (*Macronyx croceus*) also occurs among the scattered trees of open savanna.

OPPOSITE RIGHT A jewel of the bushveld, the lilacbreasted roller (*Coracias caudata*) is a relatively common sight in many game reserves. Otherwise silent, it emits a harsh chattering call during its courtship flying display.

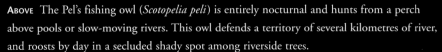

ABOVE The Pel's fishing owl (*Scotopelia peli*) is entirely nocturnal and hunts from a perch above pools or slow-moving rivers. This owl defends a territory of several kilometres of river, and roosts by day in a secluded shady spot among riverside trees.

ABOVE RIGHT The whitefaced owl (*Otus leucotis*) may nest in a well-concealed fork of a tree or an old nest of a bird of prey. This youngster will fly when it is about five weeks old.

OPPOSITE The Cape eagle owl (*Bubo capensis*) hunts spiders, reptiles and mice, but is also able to tackle birds as large as a guineafowl.

OVERLEAF LEFT AND RIGHT The nocturnal aardvark (*Oryteropus afer*), or antbear, uses its senses of smell and hearing to find termites. When digging with its powerful claws, the aardvark's ears are folded back to prevent sand entering them. Nostril hairs perform the same function.

ABOVE AND ABOVE RIGHT The large-spotted genet (*Genetta tigrina*, above) prefers the wetter regions of Africa while the small-spotted genet (*Genetta genetta*, above right) is more commonly found in the drier areas. Although very similar in both appearance and behaviour, they can be told apart. The large-spotted genet has a black tip to its tail while the tail of the small-spotted genet has a white tip. Both genets have a pronounced black band running along the spine but only the small-spotted genet can raise this band to form a crest. Both species are nocturnal and their diets consist of rodents, reptiles, insects and wild fruits.

OPPOSITE Although often referred to as the civet cat, the African civet (*Civettictus civetta*) is, in fact, related to genets and mongooses. It is absent from arid and semi-arid areas and is most often found near water. A solitary, nocturnal species, civets will feed on rodents, insects, reptiles and wild fruits as well as carrion. It marks its territory by applying scent from its anal gland on flat a face

OVERLEAF LEFT In the open, sandy areas, the springhare (*Pedetes capensis*) is common at night as it bounds along on its hindlegs with a curious movement resembling that of the kangaroo. A rodent, the springhare uses its sharp claws on its short but powerful forelimbs to dig burrows in the soft sandy soil where it sleeps during the day.

OVERLEAF RIGHT Normally silent, the presence of the lesser bushbaby (*Galago senegalensis*), or lesser galago, is usually betrayed by rustling leaves. An excellent jumper, this animal is far more comfortable in trees as it makes its way from the nest in search of tree gum, its main diet. The lesser bushbaby will also catch insects that it kills with a bite to the head. Males mark their territories – and, at times, their females – by a process known as urine washing. After urinating on its front paws, the bushbaby wipes its hands on

FAR LEFT Ever vigilant and alert, a suricate (*Suricata suricatta*), or meerkat, performs sentry duty, keeping a sharp lookout for its main enemies, the black-backed jackal and the larger eagles that prey on them.

LEFT Affectionate and playful, youngsters play at the entrance to the burrow before setting off with their parents to forage for food. Their diet consists of grubs, scorpions, lizards and insects. They will also kill and eat snakes and have an incredible tolerance for the venom of snakes and scorpions.

BOTTOM LEFT As their body temperatures rise, meerkats will spend time grooming one another. This serves not only to rid each other of fleas and parasites, but also strengthens ties between members of the group.

OPPOSITE Found only in southern Africa, the meerkat is one of the most enchanting animals of the drier regions. Meerkats live in burrows in colonies or family groups that can have up to 30 members.

OPPOSITE Meerkats only emerge from their burrows when the temperature is fairly high and gather at the entrance to sunbathe.
ABOVE The meerkat's phenomenal eyesight enables it to detect and identify a potentially dangerous raptor at a great distance and sound a warning to others in the group.

ABOVE Meerkats have an extensive home range with several burrow systems and boltholes for a quick getaway should danger threaten the safety of the group.

LEFT The yellow mongoose (*Cynictis penicillata*) often shares the meerkat's burrow system. This mongoose can be identified by its yellow coat and eyes and the white tip of its tail. Like meerkats, they are alert and active, and are capable of great speed when required.

ABOVE Young mongooses are born in the summer months and, when old enough, will accompany their mother on foraging expeditions.

OPPOSITE The smallest of the mongoose species is the dwarf mongoose (*Helogale parvula*). From their homes in old termite mounds, these intelligent, inquisitive animals set off to find food, and constantly call to one another. Only the group's dominant male and female will breed. 'Babysitters' are appointed to care for the young when the rest of the group is foraging.

OVERLEAF The ground squirrel (*Xerus inauris*) is often found sharing burrows with meerkats and yellow mongooses. A striking feature of the ground squirrel is its huge bushy tail that it raises over its back and head to act as a parasol, protecting it from the harsh African sun.